Finding CHRIST

SPIRIT REIGN
PUBLISHING
A Division of Spirit Reign Communications

ANDREA TRUSTY KING

Author: Dr. Andrea Trusty King
Cover design: David Anderson
Page design & layout: Ornan Anthony of OA.Blueprints, LLC
Editor: Dr. Ramona Hyman

Printed in the United States of America

ISBN PB: 978-1-940002-34-7
ISBN ePUB: 978-1-940002-35-4
ISBN ePDF: 978-1-940002-36-1

SPIRIT REIGN
PUBLISHING
A Division of Spirit Reign Communications

CONTENTS

ACKNOWLEDGEMENTS

Every time I think of you, I give thanks to my God, (Philippians 1:3).

Someone said, "Teamwork makes the dream work." This book would not be possible without the help, prayers and support of so many.

The most important part of the team was God and I am so grateful He allowed and empowered me to write this book. I pray many are blessed as a result of it.

I would also like to thank my husband and partner in life and ministry, Pastor Kurt King, for his undying love, support, anointing, and covering. You are an awesome man of God by whom I have been undeservingly blessed. I would also like to thank my children, Lauryn and Jonathan, who continue to inspire me and bring me joy.

I must thank my family. I am grateful to my mother, Juanita Trusty, for her inspiring example of generosity, determination and Christ's love. I am thankful to my father, Apostle David Trusty, who has given me an awesome spiritual inheritance and displays daily the supernatural power of God. Thank you to my sister, Pastor Alicia Jones—a bold, anointed woman of God who inspires me and pushes me in the Spirit. I'd also like to thank David, Ruthie, Maxinedianne and Charles for being great siblings and for tolerating me as a big sister. Many thanks to my father-in-love, Dr. George King and my mother-in-love, Germyn King for their love, prayers, support and continued encouragement.

Thank you to Barbara White who for 15 years always greeted me with, "Did you finish that book yet?" I am finally happy to report, "YES!" Thanks for believing in me.

Thank you to Jeremy Anderson and the Spirit Reign team that helped make this book a reality. Thank you to Pastor Courtney Ray and Dr. Ramona Hyman for helping to edit this manuscript.

Thank you to the many churches that have allowed me to minister with them over the years: San Diego 31st Street, San Diego Maranatha, Valley Fellowship in Rialto, CA, Imani Praise Fellowship in Moreno Valley, CA and the 16th Street Church in San Bernardino, CA, where I currently pastor.

There are a myriad of others who have helped to shape, lead, guide and grow me. Although I cannot list all of their names, for that would be a book by itself, I am eternally grateful.

INTRODUCTION

Don't understand the price heaven paid
The value heaven laid
At our feet
Salvation so sweet

That Jesus died—laid His life down
Gave up the glory of heaven
To take up my crown
Of thorns and pain
Of sin and shame
So that my name
Could be written in the Book of Life

He lived as I couldn't
Gave me access to what I shouldn't
Have access to.
Freedom and life
Riches of Christ
Erased past
And future bright

How can this be?
Christ died for me
And rose with the key
To hell, death and the grave

New joy, new life, new hope, He gave
Still can't believe it was me He saved
And what's crazy—He's not even through
Cause now He's trying to give this blessing to you.

I am praying you are blessed and that you discover the greatest blessing of all—Jesus Christ. I prayed that God would put this book into your hands and He has answered that prayer. I am sure there are other prayers God will answer as you take this journey with Him. God says to you, *"Call to Me, and I will answer you, and show you great and mighty things, which you do not know"* (Jeremiah 33:3, NKJV).

Andrea Trusty King

CHAPTER 1

FINDING JESUS

Some time ago, I had a little scare, when I lost my son in the mall. We went as a family to have our portraits taken. While we waited for the pictures to be edited, I went shopping, and my husband went to listen to a football game in the car. The kids decided to come with me.

I looked at purses and grabbed some blouses, and my daughter picked up a few accessories she wanted to buy. I noticed that my son was unusually quiet, so I turned to ask his opinion, but discovered he was no longer beside me! I went back to the belt display but he wasn't there either. I casually asked a sales associate if she had seen a little boy who was all dressed up wandering around the store. She hadn't seen him.

I walked through the entire bottom floor of the department store and called his name. There was no sign of him. The sales clerk paged him on the store's intercom and I left my daughter at the shoe counter in case he came back looking for us. I walked around the store again, this time calling a little louder, but still not trying to disturb the shoppers at the perfume counters. I made my way back to the shoes, but we still hadn't found him.

I didn't want to tell my husband that I had lost our son, but I needed help. I frantically raced through the store, praying as I yelled my son's name. Tears welled in my eyes and every horrible movie where the family didn't live "happily ever after" flooded my mind. People looked at me with indignation as I screamed his name. I looked back at them like a mother robbed of her cub. I didn't care what they thought, because I was in hot pursuit of my child. The sales clerk continued to page him, as other workers assembled in the shoe department awaiting direction. I was two seconds away from telling the manager to lock down the store: CODE KING was about to be in effect!

Just then, I got a text from my husband saying he found him. They were on the second floor. I flew up the escalator to give that little boy a piece of my mind. It never occurred to me that he would go up the escalator. And he hadn't stopped there: he went out of the store and made his way through the parking lot. I was livid!

With a sullen face and puffy red eyes, he explained that because he didn't know which way I had gone, he went to be with his father in the car. His answer made a lot of sense and rebuked me—making me feel like a horrible mother.

LOSING JESUS

I wonder if that's how Mary, the mother of Jesus felt, when she lost Him. Granted, Mary had to be a much better mother than me. When God scoured earth to find someone He could trust with His only child, He went past the kings and queens with their royal guards and wet nurses. He bypassed the philosophers, the Oprahs, the Dr. Phils, and even the Supernannies of the day to choose Mary and Joseph. They weren't perfect by men's standards, but there was something in them that made the God of the Universe honor them with heaven's most precious treasure. Yet somehow, Mary and Joseph lost Jesus.

When Jesus was twelve years old, they attended the festival as usual. After the celebration was over, they started home to Nazareth, but Jesus stayed behind in Jerusalem. His parents didn't miss Him at first, because they assumed He was among the other travelers. But when He didn't show up that evening, they started looking for Him among their relatives and friends (Luke 2:42-44).

This was perhaps Jesus' first trip to Jerusalem, His first trip to the big city. This was definitely Jesus' first Passover. Jesus had just turned twelve; by Jewish standards, that meant He was now a man. This was a momentous time because Jesus was old enough to participate in the temple rituals and customs. He was so absorbed by the Jewish holiday, that when His family departed, He was left behind. They didn't know it yet, but they had lost Jesus.

Mary and her husband went all day before they recognized Jesus was missing. Imagine their horror when they realized they had remembered to get the shoes from under the bed, they remembered to put the fire out, they remembered not to leave their toothbrushes on the sink--but they forgot Jesus! He was the reason they celebrated Passover. It was all about Jesus, but they lost sight of the most important person on the trip.

If Mary and Joseph could lose sight of what should be most important, we can too. They were so engaged in living their lives, they didn't realize they were missing Jesus until the end of the day. They were with their friends. They were laughing it up on the way home. They were talking, chatting, and traveling. So caught up with their lives, they missed the One who had come to give them life.

Mary and Joseph weren't bad parents. They had no records or incidents with Child Protective Services. As a matter of fact, I believe these two people loved Jesus more than anyone on earth. They loved Jesus, but they lost Jesus. The worse thing is that they weren't even aware that they lost Jesus. They got to the end of their journey and realized they were missing something. The best of us can lose Jesus.

The men and women usually traveled separately. The women started out a little earlier and walked at a more leisurely pace, as they had young children traveling with them. The men would meet up with the women and set up camp together. Mary probably assumed Jesus was with Joseph in the caravan of men. Joseph might have assumed that Jesus was with Mary in the caravan with the women and children.

"But when He didn't show up that evening, they started looking for Him among their relatives and friends" (Luke 2:44). They figured Jesus was with the family. They assumed that their praying mother had brought Jesus for them. They hoped their anointed aunt was walking with Jesus. Uncle Zechariah, Cousin John, their preacher friend, their missionary acquaintance—but even with all those people around, nobody had Jesus.

I can only imagine the argument heard between Mary and Joseph that night. "What do you mean it's my fault? He was supposed to be with you! It's your fault. You know the women and children travel together. You are His mother. How could you leave Him?" Joseph may have yelled.

"My fault? Oh, did you forget, we just celebrated Jesus' birthday? He's a man now. If He was a boy, He would have been traveling with me, but now that He's a man, He should have been traveling with you!" Mary might have snapped back.

I'm sure Mary and Joseph were too ashamed to pray. They would have to admit to God that they had lost His only begotten Son. Growing up, Jesus didn't have a whole lot of friends. People had been trying to kill Jesus since He was born. When Jesus was a toddler, the family had to flee the country, because King Herod, fueled by jealousy of Jesus, issued a decree to kill all the boys under two years old. Now, what if the Roman soldiers finally captured Him? What if Jesus had been kidnapped?

FINDING JESUS

Mary and Joseph couldn't get to Jerusalem for another whole day. "Mary," she tried to tell herself, "Jesus is fine. Maybe He just got caught up with some friends."

If Joseph was anything like the dads I knew growing up, he might have chimed in, "If He's with some friends—or worse yet, hugged up with some girl—forget Herod, I'm going to kill Him."

By the time they made it back to Jerusalem, they were seething. They didn't know where to begin, so they searched everywhere. They tore Jerusalem upside down. They were trying to think like a 12 year–old boy, *Where could He be?* They asked the townspeople, but no one had seen Him. They had done all they knew to do, so they would have to ask God for help. They muttered a prayer of desperation, for they couldn't do this alone. Mary pushed her way to the temple, with Joseph close beside her. As they got close, they heard a familiar voice. It was Jesus talking to the priests and rabbis. They stood by the door to listen. The boy was brilliant and had great understanding. The Bible says that He astonished the teachers and amazed His parents. The original language says they were blown away.

A wave of pride washed over Joseph and Mary. But that was quickly followed by a wave of irritation when they realized they had walked all the way back to Jerusalem! It had been over 20 miles out of the way, and they would still have to walk 70 miles home the next day. Now came a wave of anger!

Mary was annoyed now. She busted up the Bible study. If she was like my mother, she probably said, "Jesus, what is wrong with you? You had us searching all over the place for You! We left three days ago and You should have been with us! Do You know we were worried sick? You better not ever pull something like this again! Do You hear me? You had your father and I trudging all over Jerusalem praying we didn't find Your body in an alley somewhere! We've been to every arcade, park, and mall in Jerusalem looking for You!"

Jesus, undaunted and apparently not even embarrassed, simply asked, "Why were you looking for Me? Didn't you know I'd be in My Father's house? Didn't you know I would be about My Father's business?

"Just because they've said the benediction, doesn't mean church is over. Just because the crowd isn't here, the musicians put away their instruments, and the choir's gone home, doesn't mean it is finished. I don't just pick it up and lay it down. This is My life—My mission. This is what I came here for, and this is what I am about."

Jesus, though a young man, had his priorities together. When people were chatting about their bosses, Jesus was asking about the blood. When mothers were talking about their children, Jesus thirsted for knowledge about the Father. When teenagers were discussing what folks were wearing, Jesus was learning about worship. Kids His age were experimenting with the birds and the bees, but His chief concern was the blood of the Lamb. "Didn't you know I had to be about My Father's business?"

They had gotten so caught up and occupied with life, not bad things—friends, family, church—they didn't realize that Jesus was not with them. If it can happen to Mary and Joseph, how much more could it happen to us? Our lives are filled with so many things—picking up the kids from here, taking them there. We're busy calling him, meeting her, doing this project, studying for that class, working this job, paying that bill. We just assume Jesus is in the crowd, that Jesus is with our family and friends, but that won't work. Jesus is waiting for you!

The best of us can lose Jesus, but the good news is that even the worst of us can find Him. That's why Isaiah 55:6 says, *"Seek the LORD while you can find Him. Call on Him now while He is near."* God is calling us to come back to Him. Let this be a time when you get your priorities straight. Maybe you need to back track, rewind and start or renew your love relationship with Christ. That's what this book is about—looking for and finding Jesus.

Dear God, help me to get my priorities straight. Help me to put first things first. I want You to be first in my life. As I begin this journey of finding Christ, help me to find Him and follow Him forever.

CHAPTER 2

THE DAY I LOST JESUS

As I get older, things seem to disappear more often. This is in part because my children continue to move things and not put them back where they belong. As much as I would like to blame my children for everything I've lost, sometimes it has nothing to do with them and everything to do with me. I've noticed that I am getting more forgetful the older I get.

My great grandmother recently died a month shy of her one-hundredth birthday. As far back as I could remember, Grandmama, as we called her, was a senior citizen. She was diagnosed with dementia in her later years, but I am pretty sure she had a touch of it when I was growing up because she was very forgetful. She would put a pot in the bathroom and when she couldn't find it in the kitchen, she would accuse me of stealing it. From her teeth to toilet paper, if she couldn't find it, she just knew I took it.

"Where's my purple dress, Andrea?" Grandmama would ask.

"I don't know, Grandmama. I don't have it," would be my exasperated reply.

"Well, go check your suitcase. You know how you like to steal," she'd accuse.

"I don't steal, Grandmama. And I didn't steal

your dress. What did it look like? Maybe I can help you find it," I offered as a peace offering. But she wasn't buying it.

"I bet you could help me find it. It's probably in your suitcase somewhere. It was a purple dress with green fl—."

"Flowers?" I interrupted. "A purple dress with green flowers?"

"I knew you had it!" she shot back.

"No, Grandmama, you have it," I sighed. "You have it ON!"

"Well, I must have two," she snapped, "and I am sure the other one is in your suitcase."

I was undone. There was no convincing her, so I decided that I would just stay away from her. I wouldn't go to visit anymore. I figured when she saw her stuff was still missing, she would know that I wasn't taking it. During that time, we didn't see each other much because she didn't come to our house either.

There was one week that Grandmama came to visit that I will never forget. My mother was away on business and Grandmama was watching us. I was a teenager with a car and job, but not a lot of money. My friend kept getting new stuff that I knew neither one of us could afford. When I asked how she got it, she told me about her five–finger discount. She would steal it and encouraged me to try it for myself.

It just so happened that I was browsing through a store one day and I saw some perfume. I smelled it and I liked it a little bit. You know, enough to wear it sometimes, but not enough to take money out of my pocket to pay for it. While I was in the valley of decision of whether or not to buy it, I decided I would test it out. I decided to crown one of those lucky bottles as my very own tester. I'd take one that day and if I liked it, I would buy another one. It was buy one, get one free in reverse. "Who knows," I told myself, "I might become a lifelong customer."

I had never stolen anything before. The thought never occurred to me. I don't know why it occurred to me on that particular day and I sure don't know why I listened. I obviously didn't know what I was doing—which in hindsight was a good thing—because my four-minute crime spree was enough to get me straight for life.

With the bottle hidden, I headed for my car. Before I knew what was happening, I was escorted to the back of the store with Loss Recovery. That was the politically correct way of saying "The Thief Department." They were the store cops and I was in trouble. They high–fived each other behind my back and boasted, "We got another one." To this day, I still don't know what I was thinking.

I was a minor so, of course, they had to call my mother. My mother was out of town, so you know who picked up the phone. It was Grandmama. She wasn't surprised one bit to hear that I had been hauled up in some store by two rent-a-cops because I was shoplifting.

"I knew it!" She exclaimed with an air of vindication. "I bet she has on a purple dress. That's stolen too! That's my purple dress, Officer." I was mortified.

They took my picture and plastered me on the Wall of Shame. This store was popular among the people at my church. I was horrified at the thought that my picture would be up there for everyone to see. I tried to console myself that I was just like Jesus, humiliated and hanging between two thieves. But unlike Jesus, I knew the sin and shame were all mine. I felt like the Chief of Sinners.

It almost sounds blasphemous to compare myself to Jesus. Jesus was innocent. He had done no wrong. This world was stolen from Him and He simply came to take it back. He could have busted up the place or done like I did: snatched the Earth, put it in His pocket and tried to walk out. But He decided to *buy* us back. He didn't get us at a bargain either. He bought us with His blood, His life.

I remember sitting in the back room. It was a cross between a cop's desk and one of those interrogation rooms you see on TV. There was a monitor in the corner. They offered to show me what they had caught on tape. I didn't want to see that other me, that ugly me, in action. "No, thank you. I'm good," I replied, hoping to send a subliminal message that I was not the horrible thief they thought I was no matter what the video said. My eyes, my ears, my heart could not relive the moment again.

It sounds silly now, but I even offered to pay them. I told them I had the money right in my pocket. "You are going to pay alright, but keep your money for now," the skinny officer said with smugness in his voice. They ended up not pressing charges since this was my first offense. Still, the fines were well over ten times the value of the stupid perfume.

Even as a kid, I never liked to pay full price. I loved a bargain, so in my head, getting something for free was a natural progression. I learned, though, that stealing is the most costly shopping of all. In addition to being stupid and wrong, it was just plain too expensive!

There was another cost I paid that I didn't anticipate—the pain, the shame, and the embarrassment. There were hushed tones of people whispering about me. It's one thing when people talk badly about you, and they are lying. It's another thing when they talk badly about you, and they are telling the truth. What could I say? There was nothing to say, so I didn't talk for about a week.

People asked me what was wrong, but I wouldn't tell them. I couldn't disclose my ugly secret. They asked me questions and told me to nod my head, "Are you moving?"

I shook my head "No."
"Did someone die?" they urged.
I shook my head "Yes," meaning me.

READING, WRITING, AND REGRET

Quiet as it's kept, we all fail. We all make mistakes. Saved people, church people, rich people, poor people, Blacks, Whites, Latinos, Asians, gay, straight, we all mess up sometimes. To err is human. Sometimes we make little blunders and oversights, and sometimes we do things that rock us to our core.

We all aim for success. We dream of prosperity and upward mobility—but after reading, writing and arithmetic, someone should have talked about regret. After faith and forgiveness, or even physics, someone should have taught us about failure, because more people fail than succeed. Disappointments come quicker and a lot more often than destiny.

So what do you do then? What do you do when you mess up royally? The first thing you do is remember that failure isn't final, even though it often feels like it is. When you fail, it feels like forever. People may treat you like it is forever, but failure isn't final. You can get from under this thing. One day, people will look at you again and not remember what you did. You are bigger than your mishap, your misstep, your misappropriation, your misjudgment, your misunderstanding, your misfortune, your mistake.

Peter, who the Bible also calls Simon, knew what it was like to fail. The time when his best friend Jesus needed him, he left Him. Peter denied Him and acted like he didn't even know Jesus. Realizing what he had done,

Peter's face was red and swollen. His eyes were big and puffy from crying so much. His blood–shot eyes burned, but this depressed disciple had no tears left to extinguish their fire, for he had betrayed Jesus.

By now, Jesus was all grown up, far removed from celebrating His first Passover. At the young age of 33, He was celebrating His last. Jesus, usually full of joy, was acting weird to Peter. He kept saying that He was going to die. Not only would He die, but also Jesus said that His own disciples would betray and desert Him.

That's where Peter had to draw the line. He knew he was willing to die for Jesus. Peter was offended that Jesus would think his own disciples could turn their backs on Him. Jesus warned Peter he wasn't as committed as he thought he was. When the going got tough, Peter would get going. Jesus was so serious; he called Peter by his old name, Simon. *"Simon, Simon, Satan has asked to sift each of you like wheat. But I have pleaded in prayer for you, Simon, that your faith should not fail. So when you have repented and turned to Me again, strengthen your brothers"* (Luke 22:31–32).

It was nice that Jesus warned Peter that the devil was asking for permission to tear him apart. What would have been nicer was Jesus telling Satan, "No. You cannot sift Simon Peter. He is my disciple!" I suppose Peter should have been grateful that Jesus prayed for him, but Jesus didn't pray that Peter wouldn't be sifted, or even that he wouldn't fail. Jesus prayed that Peter's faith wouldn't fail.

When the soldiers came to take Jesus, as Peter promised, he fought back. Peter started swinging his sword. He was trying to take off a man's head, but only got his ear. Jesus walked up to the man. *"Now he's going to get it,"* Peter thought, but Jesus didn't hit him; He healed him! With that, Peter ran before Jesus got them all killed. From then on, he denied he even knew Jesus. The crowing of the rooster reminded Peter of his conversation with Jesus. Peter realized he failed and wondered if Jesus was still praying that his faith wouldn't.

It was as if Jesus was saying, "Look, I know you are going to fail, but don't let your faith fail. Even if you give up on yourself, don't give up on Me. The system or schools may fail. Your marriage or health may fail. Your parents or spouse may fail, but don't let your faith fail. When you stop believing in yourself, still believe in Me. When you realize that you can't, don't stop trusting that I can."

Jesus' point was if you are going to get through your failures, past your mistakes, and over your guilt—you can't let your faith fail, when you fail. Jesus was reminding Peter that there would be some situations that would come, some winds and waves, some trials and tribulations, some mistakes and missteps. All those things come from the outside, but Jesus was looking for the opportunity to put something on the *inside* of Peter that would help him when he couldn't help himself.

After my shoplifting incident, I remember feeling like an utter failure. I had spent my whole life trying to convince the world (and Grandmama) that I was not a thief. Yet, I had become the thing I vowed never to be! After that, I didn't want to be around people. I remember going down to the basement and curling up in a closet. Away from the world, surrounded by the darkness I was sure I deserved, I cried. I sobbed. I berated myself with how dumb, stupid, cheap, and maybe even evil, I was. I was done with myself, the world… everything!

I prayed to God for forgiveness, but I assumed my calls went straight to voicemail. I was sure He was through with me. I begged and pleaded, snotted and cried. I wanted God to see how sorry I was, but I was sure He was not interested. I was sure that I had lost Jesus.

Although I refused to come out of that dark closet, a light came in and I felt something hug me. I felt love and joy and peace and forgiveness flood the room. I felt valuable. Loved. Forgiven. It was in the dark of the closet that I saw the light of Christ. I made a vow then to tell anybody who walked by that closet how good God was. I had a burning desire to tell someone how much love God has even when we mess up. "God," I sobbed between breaths, "thank you for loving me! I would tell others of Your forgiveness, if they were here. I promise, God, I'm going to tell people how You saved me and that You want to save them too." It was like Jesus' words to Peter were written for me, *"So when you have repented and turned to Me again, strengthen your brothers"* (Luke 22:32). Though I failed and felt like I lost Jesus, when I turned to Him, I found He was right beside me.

In the same way Jesus prayed for Peter, I believe He prays for you and me. Hebrews 7:25 tells us, *"Therefore He is able to save completely those who come to God through Him, because He always lives to intercede for them."* There are some of you who are reading this book who have made mistakes and missteps. You wonder if God will love you, if God can change you, if He can forgive you. I am so glad to report that God can and God will.

"But you don't know what I've done!" you may protest. It doesn't matter what you've done. As you will soon find out, it's about all that He has done. I'm convinced your badness is no match for His goodness. Jesus is praying for you right now to repent, turn from your mistakes, and turn to Him. He wants to show you what great love He has for you.

Dear God, thank You for the love You have for me. Forgive me for the times I have failed and messed up. I want to get close to You and experience Your love. Help me, God. I need You!

CHAPTER 3

LOST IN TRANSLATION

My father and I were preaching in Uganda some time ago. We didn't speak Ugandan, so we had to have an interpreter translate our messages. I remember during a particular sermon, my father was pouring out his heart to the Ugandan people, sharing how much God loved them and how He wanted to save them. In that intense moment, the crowd erupted in laughter. I gasped because I didn't understand what was happening. Apparently neither did the translator. The sermon was about the Messiah, but he shouted something about monkeys. Something was lost in translation.

Although it wasn't funny to me then, it can be a little comical when words and meanings get lost in translation. When Kentucky Fried Chicken went to China in the late 80's, the company wanted to translate its slogan "Finger-licking good" into Mandarin. Something was lost in translation, and the slogan was translated, "We'll eat your fingers off." Pepsi did no better during its transition into the Chinese market. Their team translated the slogan, "Pepsi Brings You Back to Life" pretty literally. In Chinese, it read, "Pepsi Brings Your Ancestors Back from the Grave!" When Coca-Cola first went to China, the soft drink was named something that sounded like "Coca-Cola." The only problem was the characters used meant "Bite the Wax Tadpole." The intended meaning was lost in translation. My favorite "lost in translation" moment came from Coors. Their slogan is, "Turn It Loose." But when it was translated into Spanish, their billboards read "Suffer From Diarrhea!" Talk about lost in translation!

I wish these misunderstandings only happen occasionally, or with a select few. But there are many instances when there is a failure to communicate. This doesn't just happen between people; it even happens with God. Don't be confused; God does not have a problem with His communication skills. Sometimes we have a problem in our listening or understanding skills. The Bible says in Isaiah 55:8-9 that God's ways and thoughts are nothing like ours. Like heaven is higher than earth, God's thoughts are higher than our thoughts.

Still, that doesn't stop God from trying to communicate with us. As a matter of fact, it probably makes God try harder! The record clearly shows, God has gone to great lengths to show His great love, but somehow it has gotten lost in translation.

BACK TO EDEN

Let's look back to the Garden of Eden. Imagine what it would have looked like before death began to brown bright petals and make young leaves turn limp. Imagine the splendor before there were thorns that popped out like pimples on flowers and trees; before weeds pirated gardens snatching up nutrients and water from the rightful good plants. Imagine Eden with all of its beauty. I am sure it was heaven on earth! Gold and gems lined the place. Rivers ran through the land like children on a summer day. God made every pleasure imaginable for Adam and Eve. Fruits and flowers, trees and treasures were all made for their enjoyment. Best of all, they were able to take quiet walks with the Creator of the Universe.

God outdid Himself! I imagine He told Adam and Eve something like, "You can have all of this. I did this for you to show you My great love! Eat from the cherry and the mulberry tree, the pomegranate and the peach tree, the banana and the coconut tree, the apricot and the apple tree. When you get bored with all of those, there are hundreds of other trees for you to explore and enjoy. As a matter of fact, you can have all the trees on the whole earth! They are all yours—all but the tree of the knowledge of good and evil. Don't touch that one for it is Mine. It will make you see things you don't want to see. Take My word for it and leave that tree alone for its fruit will kill you. If you eat it, you will surely die."

Somehow God's message of love was lost in translation. Adam and Eve ignored all the wonderful creations they *could* have and began to hone in on the one thing God had forbidden. "God is trying to keep something from us. Let's taste some of that forbidden fruit so our eyes will be opened," they may have mused.

Perhaps you know the story. When Adam and Eve ate

the fruit, their eyes were open. However, by rebelling against God, they released sin and rebellion all over the world. We still cringe at the bitter aftertaste of sin and death today.

Still in His mercy, God didn't leave us without a clue on how to brave this new dangerous world. He gave us His law to help us steer clear of unnecessary trouble. He gave us guidelines to help keep us out of harm's way, but we didn't see it like that. We thought God was trying to keep something from us—that He was trying to steal our freedom. No, He was trying to keep us out of jail, to protect us from baby mama drama, and to shield us from other pains and heartaches.

He decided to send us a love letter through the Bible, so we could read it over and over again. There should have been no confusion after we read of His everlasting love, His unfailing mercy, and His unlimited grace. He gave dreams and visions to the prophets. They stood up and declared the word of God to the people. Still, the message didn't always get through.

"So the Word became human and made His home among us. He was full of unfailing love and faithfulness. And we have seen His glory, the glory of the Father's one and only Son" (John 1:14). God grew tired of trying to get our attention by dividing the Red Sea and making the sun go backwards. He used floods and even rained down fire from heaven. He made the lame walk and donkeys talk. He did everything short of coming here Himself. So He did that, too.

God wouldn't sit high and look low anymore. He was tired of His love getting lost in translation. God was weary of *sending* messages, so He *became* the message. The Word jumped out of a book and into a body. The Word became human.

Jesus said farewell to His Father and the angels. He arose from His throne, and began to walk the golden streets. He didn't stop at the Tree of Life like He used to, because this time He was going to taste death. The happiness and joy of heaven, the power and glory from above—He gave it all up. He shed his garments of glory and wrapped Himself in human flesh. He who formed it with His own hands crawled into the womb of a woman. The Sun of Righteousness, the Light of the World entered this dark earth. Jesus came to this world to reveal God's great love for humanity. God went through great lengths to show His great love.

Dear God, thank You for Your great love for me. Forgive me for the times I misunderstood You and decided to do things my own way, rather than Your way. Thank you for sending Your Son, Jesus, to earth to die for my sins. I accept Him today as my Savior.

CHAPTER 4

EVERYDAY PEOPLE, EXTRAORDINARY JESUS

When Jesus walked the earth and was with people—real people, everyday people, like you and me—He began to minister to them. He would meet people plagued by guilt and shame; people haunted by their pasts and would tell them, *"Your sins are forgiven you."* Jesus wanted humanity to know, *"If we confess our sins to Him, He is faithful and just to forgive us our sins and to cleanse us from all wickedness"* (1 John 1:9). Jesus is a forgiver.

John 8 tells the story of Jesus teaching in the temple courtyard one day. Meanwhile across town, some church leaders caught a woman in the very act of adultery. They yanked her out of the bed, dragged her through the streets and threw her in front of Jesus. She clung to a tattered blanket to cover herself and to keep the last ounce of dignity she had left. Mothers covered their sons' eyes, and gave their husbands a poke coupled with a look that said, "You better look at Jesus and not at that naked woman!"

The law said that this woman should die. The church leaders demanded to know what Jesus was going to do. Jesus began to write in the sand. Without saying a word, He communicated, "You are right; the law says she should die, but she isn't the only one. I know what you did last summer. I know what you did last night. So who's going to throw the first stone? Who's bad enough? Rather, who's good enough? Whoever doesn't live in a glass house, go ahead, start throwing stones."

Jesus didn't name any names, but everybody with stones in their hands realized they had no business in her business. Jesus was the only one who could stone her, but He decided to deliver her from certain death and restore her to abundant life. He said, "Woman, I don't condemn you. Go and sin no more." Jesus is a deliverer.

Not only is Jesus a forgiver and a deliverer, but He is also the Master. We don't like that. We don't like for anyone to tell us what to do. We don't mind a savior or healer but we really don't want a master. What many people don't realize is we are going to serve somebody. We either serve God or Satan. There is no middle ground.

Quiet as it's kept, the devil is a hard taskmaster. People don't tell the whole truth when they describe their lives of sin. I have heard testimonies where people act like they had so much fun at the party or with the person they met at the club. They don't want to reveal how stupid they felt when they woke up alone, or how horrible they felt when they were hungover. They don't like to tell about the voices that torment them, the crying spells, the times they wanted to die, the times they almost died. They learned from experience that serving the devil comes with a high price tag.

Jesus knows when we choose to serve other gods, we get messed up and lose out on the joy and peace He has for us. That's why Jesus makes us an offer we can't refuse. He reassures, "I have come to deliver you from the drama, the darkness, the pain, and the shame."

You mean the world to God. You were bought with a price; the receipt is still dripping with the blood of Jesus. And He promised that God, the One who started this good work in you, will keep on working in your life until you are complete in Him. That means when you give your life to Christ, He will begin to make you into a wonderful new creation. He will continue sculpting His masterpiece in your life until He comes again.

Today, Jesus offers you salvation and the opportunity to be His follower. He is ready, willing and able to take you, to change you, and to transform you into the very best person you can be. Will you receive Christ's offer—His sacrifice for your salvation, His death for your new life? If you have not accepted Jesus as your Lord and Savior, this is your opportunity. There are two options: good or evil; God or Satan; God's way or the world's way; heaven or hell. Today you need to decide whose side you will take.

What does it mean to be on the Lord's side? It means He becomes the most important person in your life.

The Lord becomes your Master and you are His follower. It means that effective immediately you begin living your life His way.

I pray you make one of the most important and rewarding decisions of your life—that you decide to become one of Jesus' followers. This is a lifelong journey that God promises to take with you. He promises that He will never leave you nor forsake you. God has started something good in your life, and He promises that He will finish what He started. I can't promise the road will always be easy, but keep reading. You are about to find out how to keep going, even when you want to give up.

If you want to commit to becoming a follower of Christ, pray this prayer:

Father, thank You for sending Jesus to die for my sins. I understand that Jesus is Your Son and the only way to You. I want Jesus to be Lord of my life and I want to be His lifelong follower. By Your grace, I accept the free gift of salvation through faith, in the Name of Jesus, Amen.

CHAPTER 5

LOOK AND LIVE

Have you ever been mad at God? I remember when my husband and I were at seminary studying to become pastors. We were rich in love but poor in just about everything else. We had five jobs between the two of us and still lived below the poverty line. Yet, the time was remarkable because we saw God do wonderful things in our lives and in the lives of others as a result of our prayers.

Those times of miracles and answered prayer made the five jobs and the food bank meals all worthwhile—until I became ill. I didn't have health insurance, so I couldn't afford the procedures or the prescriptions. I didn't get better, so I couldn't work, which meant less money for food, tuition, rent, utilities or medical bills. It was a vicious cycle that turned downward quickly.

I kept my spirits up for a little while. However, the days turned into weeks, and I could do nothing but lie in the bed and pray. I think that is when the anger came. I had too much time to think of the people who I had seen God heal. I reflected on all of the miracles that happened for other people when I prayed for them. But when I prayed for myself, I got nothing: no healing, no help. Here I was working and sacrificing for the Lord, but when I needed Him, He didn't seem to answer. I expected God to come through for me, like I had seen Him come through for others, but I was still sick, still sad and even a little mad at God.

I was disappointed with God and discouraged with life. Disappointment is a tricky thing. It's a gateway drug that opens the door to discouragement. Discouragement is where you lose your will to press through hard times. You look at your past and present and dread your future. Discouraged is what I was then, and that is what some of us are right now.

That is definitely what the children of Israel were. They had spent almost 40 years wandering in the desert. The trip from Egypt to Canaan should have taken two weeks. It had been almost four decades and these former slaves had not reached the Promised Land. It seemed as if the children of Israel would never arrive. They were tired and didn't think they could go any further.

Numbers 21:4–5 says, *"Then they journeyed from Mount Hor by the Way of the Red Sea, to go around the land of Edom; and the soul of the people became very discouraged on the way. And the people spoke against God and against Moses: "Why have you brought us up out of Egypt to die in the wilderness? For there is no food and no water, and our soul loathes this worthless bread"* (NKJV).

God had blessed the children of Israel and kept them all these years; instead of commending God, they criticized Him. Instead of gratitude, there was grumbling.

They didn't understand that complaining was the devil's praise.

We do the same thing. Instead of talking about what God has done, we talk about what the devil has done. Instead of looking to Jesus, we look at our problems. Instead of focusing on our wonderful Savior, we focus on our terrible situations. We choose to overlook the blessings God has given us.

The Israelites took it a step further. Not only did they overlook the blessings of God, they *despised* them. God gave them manna, which the Bible says was angels' food. He performed a miracle for them every morning by emptying out barrels of bread from heaven's pantry, and that miracle made them mad.

It is dangerous to despise the blessings of God, and we do it all too often. Perhaps you prayed for the job you have. You had your friends and family pray that you would get this job. Now that you have gotten the job, you can't stand it. You want to quit because it wasn't what you expected. You despise the blessings of God. What you desired you now detest.

I have seen it time and time again. A woman prays to find a husband, and when a man comes along, she is sure God sent him. It was as if a tag hung from his ear that read, "From God, With Love." He was the answer to all her prayers, but now she can't stand him. "How long, O Lord, is forever?" she questions. "How long, O

God, till death do us part?" she wonders. That is despising the blessings of God.

Israel complained about God, His servant, Moses, and the miracle of manna. God was protecting them and keeping them, but they neglected to realize it, so God removed the restraining order He placed on the snakes and serpents. He allowed them free range. They began to bite the people, and many of them died in the wilderness.

It didn't take long for the Israelites to realize they were no match for the serpents. They realized that they had sinned. They realized they had spoken out of turn. They began to remember the blessings of God. They missed His protection, and they repented.

CHANGE YOUR MIND

To repent is to be sorry about your sin and to turn from it. In the Bible's original language, one of the meanings of "repent" is to change your mind. The people of Israel changed their mind about God and Moses. They were sorry for what they had said and for the punishment they had received. They realized what they had done wrong. *"Then the people came to Moses and cried out, 'We have sinned by speaking against the LORD and against you. Pray that the LORD will take away the snakes.' So Moses prayed for the people"* (Numbers 21:7).

Some people think repentance is only understanding that something is wrong. It is far more than that because we can know something is wrong, and do it anyway. There is a song that says, "If loving you is wrong, I don't want to be right." Repentance is realizing that what you've been doing is wrong and deciding you want to be right. It is being sorry for what you have done, not just sorry about consequences, or getting caught, or going to jail. You are sorry that you caused God pain, and you want Him to forgive you and to help you not to make the same bad choices again.

Repentance is not just about changing your mind, but it is also about changing your direction. The people wanted Moses to pray that God would take away the serpents. They wanted the consequences of their actions removed, but God did not answer that prayer, and He seldom does. He forgives the sin, but He often leaves the consequences.

Many times, we want deliverance. We want God to pull us out of our mess quickly. We want God to make it all go away. We want Him to erase our mistake from everyone's memory. We want to be unfired. We want to get our job back. We want our virginity back. We want God to push the Divine Delete button and make everything better. Often, God doesn't pull us from the mess; instead, He helps us *through* the mess.

The Bible does not say that God took away the serpents—what He did was provide a way of escape. He didn't take away the opportunity to get bitten. Instead, He provided a prescription for those who were bitten.

God told Moses to make a bronze serpent, just like the one that had bitten the people. He told him to put it on a pole, lift it up, and everyone who looked at the serpent would be healed. The people were already sorry. They changed their minds, and now God was going to help them change their direction. They had turned from their ungratefulness and complaining. They had stopped speaking against God and Moses, and they asked Moses to speak to God on their behalf. I believe it was after Moses prayed that they were able to change their direction. God called them to turn from the problem and look towards Him. All they had to do was look, and they would live.

Although they didn't know it then, they were looking at more than just a present prescription. God was giving them a peak into the future of what would be an eternal cure not just for snake bites, but for our hearts and souls. Jesus said, *"And as Moses lifted up the bronze snake on a pole in the wilderness, so the Son of Man must be lifted up, so that everyone who believes in Him will have eternal life"* (John 3:14–15).

CURE FOR THE SIN–SICK SOUL

Serpents, which often represent sin in the Bible, have been messing us up since the Garden of Eden. It's like sin keeps biting us and leaving its mark. The Bible says, *"For everyone has sinned; we all fall short of God's glorious standard"* (Romans 3:23). The wages of sin is death, so that means the bite is fatal. Unless we get a prescription, or some antivenin to counteract the poison, we will die eternally. Antivenin is made from blood. To make it, snake poison is injected into a lamb. The lamb's body makes antibodies to shield him from the poison. Scientists take the blood of the lamb and extract the antibodies that get rid of the snake's poison.

"For without the shedding of blood, there is no forgiveness" (Hebrews 9:22). In order to save the snake–bit and sin–sick soul, God needed blood, but not just any blood would do. He needed blood from the Lamb. He needed powerful and precious blood, cleansing and wonder–working blood. He needed blood that could be contaminated with the poison but still conquer the poison. Jesus Christ, the Son of God and the Son of Man, offered His blood. *"Look! The Lamb of God, which takes away the sins of the world"* (John 1:29).

This great dragon—the ancient serpent called the devil, or Satan, the one deceiving the whole world—was thrown down to the earth with all his angels. Then I heard a loud voice shouting across the heavens, "It has come at last—salvation and power and the Kingdom of our God, and the authority of His Christ. For the accuser of our brothers and sisters has been thrown down to earth— the one who accuses them before our God day and night. And ***they have defeated him by the blood of the Lamb*** *and by their testimony. And they did not love their lives so much that they were afraid to die* (Revelation 12:9-11).

John prophesied in Revelation that we would have victory over the serpent through the blood of the Lamb!

Even when that old serpent, Satan, tries to bite us, we do not have to fall prey to him. Jesus came to give us victory over Satan and to destroy all his works in our lives. First John 3:8 says, *"But the Son of God came to destroy the works of the devil."* Jesus came to heal us of our sins and sent the Spirit to empower us for a life of victory.

"And as Moses lifted up the bronze snake on a pole in the wilderness, so the Son of Man must be lifted up, so that everyone who believes in Him will have eternal life" (John 3:14–15). Jesus compared Himself to that serpent in the wilderness, and I didn't like that too much. Serpents are sly, slick and slimy. We associate snakes with the devil and sin. It is offensive to me that Jesus would compare Himself to a nasty old serpent. Why not a peacock with all of its glory? Why not a dove with its spiritual implications? How about an eagle with its ability to soar above the storm?

Why a serpent? The Bible says He who never sinned, actually *became* sin to deliver us from it. Second Corinthians 5:21 says, *"God made Him who had no sin to be sin for us, so that in Him we might become the righteousness of God"* (NIV). He became a curse to provide a cure for the curse. Galatians 3:13 says, *"Christ redeemed us from the curse of the law by becoming a curse for us, for it is written: 'Cursed is everyone who is hung on a pole'"* (NIV).

I remember watching the news in horror during the Easter season. The reporter told of a Filipino festival where people were crucified. Participants would feel real nails in their hands and in their feet. The guards would leave them on the cross for 10 minutes. They were crucified for their sins! Others were beaten with whips that had glass and nails on the ends. The story showcased a man who had been crucified 17 times. When the reporter asked those who were crucified why they did it, they answered that they were atoning for their sins.

It hurt my heart to watch them go through this unnecessary torture because Jesus gave His back for our stripes, His head for our thorns, His side for our spear, His hands for our nails. He gave up His crown for our cross. Jesus died a horrible death, so we could have abundant life.

There is power in His blood. When those at the festival shed their blood, it didn't do anything for them. For the man that had to be crucified 17 times, that should have been evident. King David says of God, *"For You do not desire sacrifice, or else I would give it; You do not delight in burnt offering" (Psalm 51:16). Hebrews 10:10 says, "For God's will was for us to be made holy by the sacrifice of the body of Jesus Christ,* ***once for all time****."* (**emphasis added**).

Jesus died once and that sacrifice was powerful enough to save us for all time. One Lord, one faith, one baptism, one grace, one Savior, one sacrifice, one prescription, one cure. Jesus Christ is the one and only way. He is willing to save from the utttermost to the guttermost.

Do you, like the people of Israel, need to repent of your sins? Do you need to change your mind and your direction? If so, pray this prayer of repentance:

Father, in times of my discouragement, help me to look to You. Forgive me for the times I have complained and not appreciated the things You have done for me. Thank You for the many blessings You send my way every day. And thank You for Jesus' sacrifice which brings forgiveness for my sins.

CHAPTER 6

THE FREEDOM OF FORGIVENESS

Recently, I got a speeding ticket. It was the first speeding ticket I had gotten since I was in high school. I was taking my kids to school, and we were running a little late. I was coming down a hill in a group of cars. There was a police officer on a bike, hiding behind an SUV. He pulled out behind me, the last car in the caravan. I was caught!

While the officer was writing my citation, my mind wondered how much money the ticket would cost. Money was already low. I did not have an extra $600 to give the city. Instead of venting out loud or letting my imagination get the best of me, I decided to turn this into a teachable moment for my kids.

"So what did we learn from this experience?" I asked. Admittedly, I was hoping for answers like "Let's get ready for school on time, so Mommy doesn't have to speed," or "Even when you are late, you should still honor the speed limit." I would have settled for "When you do wrong, you won't get away with it."

My daughter replied, "I learned to never let Mommy drive you to school, because she is going to get a ticket."

Not to be outdone, my son shared the wisdom he gleaned from this situation, "I learned to ride with Daddy; he drives way faster, but he knows how to not get caught."

I now struggled with the lesson I would take away. My children were disappointed that I did not know how to get away with speeding since everyone does it. As I reentered the flow of traffic and we all coasted above the speed limit, I felt a twinge of guilt.

Looking back, I didn't apologize to the officer or admit that I was wrong. Actually, I tried to correct him. There was a speedometer posted on the street, and it said I was going 4 miles slower than he accused me of going. I was not sorry about speeding. I was sorry I had to pay a ticket and my children were sorry I was caught. I think that day I learned how NOT to repent!

BABY MAMA DRAMA

For a better example, let's turn to the Bible. A story is told of King David. He had just gotten word that Bathsheba, the woman he was sleeping with, was pregnant. The problem was that they were both married to other people. David was a powerful man who had the resources to cover this scandal up and that's exactly what he did. In a government conspiracy, David had Bathsheba's husband killed. Not long after, the government chariot rolled up to his mistress' home with a rehearsed speech that might have started with the words, "We regret to inform you. . . ."

Now that Uriah was out of the way, David took Uriah's wife as his own and carried on like nothing had happened. David still showed up for church and sang in the temple. He still donned that kingly smile. Bathsheba worked that first lady hat. And no one said a word.

Eventually the secret got out, and God began to deal with David. Although he was filled with regret, David was also filled with relief because the secrets took a toll on him. The nightmares he had about Uriah never seemed to end. Once he knew his sin was out in the open, he was able to go to God and ask Him for forgiveness. David was beginning the process of repentance. Even though it was a hard road, he found it led to the blessing of freedom and forgiveness.

Festo Kivengere, a bishop in Uganda during the East African revival, remembers a man who experienced that same freedom and forgiveness. When Christianity first came to his village, many people thought it was a strange, silly religion. That was until a wealthy man who was known to be into witchcraft brought the chief 8 cows. The man confessed that he had stolen the cows from the chief, but since he had found Jesus, he wanted to return them. Everyone was nervously silent as they waited to see what would happen to this criminal, but the man looked unafraid. He explained, "You can put me in prison, sir, or have me beaten. I deserve it. But I am at peace and a free man for the first time." The chief could see the joy he had. It puzzled him so much; he decided to let the man go. When Bishop Kivengere asked the chief, who was also his uncle, if he was happy about the free cows, he revealed he wasn't. The chief confessed he would have to return a hundred cows to have the joy and peace that man had. The chief coveted the freedom of the converted man. That wealthy man found new riches—the blessings of forgiveness.

David knew about blessings. Ever since he was a boy, he had been blessed and highly favored. As king of Israel, he was at the height of his career. He didn't have people trying to kill him. He didn't have to fight all the time. He wasn't living in the wilderness. God had given him peace. He had the palace, position, prosperity, and posterity. David had it going on. In light of all these blessings, David still decided that if he were to brag about anything, it would be about the blessing of forgiveness, renewal, and the joy that comes with repentance.

David had gotten to a place where he was willing to give up all the other stuff for peace. This king had a royal house, but he really wanted happiness. He got the job, but he was beginning to miss the joy. The Lamborghini didn't mean that much to him, not when he was lacking in love. He couldn't be concerned with Prada; he needed pardon.

Oh, what joy for those whose disobedience is forgiven, whose sin is put out of sight! Yes, what joy for those whose record the LORD has cleared of guilt, whose lives are lived in complete honesty! When I refused to confess my sin, my body wasted away, and I groaned all day long. Day and night Your hand of discipline was heavy on me. My strength evaporated like water in the summer heat. Finally, I confessed all my sins to You and stopped trying to hide my guilt. I said to myself, "I will confess my rebellion to the LORD." And You forgave me! All my guilt is gone (Psalm 32:1-5).

David compares the pain of his guilt with the prize of his forgiveness. He admits that on the outside he appeared as if everything was okay. However, on the inside, while he was in sin, he was wasting away. The scandal sapped his strength. God's hand was heavy on David. Although God was trying to get him back on the right path, for a long time, David refused.

King David wanted to live in his sin. The wages of sin is death, the guilt of sin is heavy, and the consequence of sins is hard. When we release our sin and allow God to take them from us, we will find relief. If we continue to hold on to our sins, we have to bear them alone. We aren't big enough or bad enough to bear our own sins. Our arms aren't long enough, our legs aren't quick enough, and our backs aren't strong enough to bear the heavy burden of our guilt. We will be crushed by the weight of it. David could feel death coming upon him. His body was growing old and dying on him.

His only option was to confess and acknowledge his sins to God. This is a key step because sometimes we can do wrong for so long that we begin to think that what we're doing is right. We don't want to acknowledge our actions as sins, so we begin to rationalize them. The first few times we feel bad and we promise to never do "it" again. But when we do it again (and again), sometimes we decide that since we aren't going to change what we're doing; we will just change our view about what we're doing.

When we acknowledge our sins to God, He forgives us and gives us freedom! There is a relief that releases us from guilt and shame. When David stopped trying to hide his sin and confessed it to God, it was washed away. His guilt was gone, and he finally had joy!

SEEK WHILE YOU CAN FIND

After David tells us what happened to him, he offers some instructions. He tells us how he got up, so if we ever get down, we would know that we don't have to stay there. What was David's prescription? David prayed and praised.

"Therefore let all the faithful pray to you while you may be found; surely the rising of the mighty waters will not reach them" (Psalm 32:6, NIV). David instructs us to pray while God is found. Does that mean God is hiding from us? No. This verse speaks far more about us than it does about God. There are times when we are more prone to listen to God. We hear God speaking to our hearts and feel His hand heavy on us. Sometimes we feel our hearts pound or our stomachs churn. We know there is something going on inside, and we can feel it. Our heart is being softened and that is our time of finding.

The Bible says God grants repentance (2 Timothy 2:25). Jesus says no one comes to Him unless the Father draws him (John 6:44). Heaven is doing all it can to aid in our repentance. When you feel the pull of repentance, act on it. When you feel sorry for your sin and feel the urge to do better, know that God is near. When you feel the Holy Spirit tugging on your heart, repent, turn from your past sin, and pray that God will keep you from future sin. Don't wait; act immediately! Many people think they will be able to start living right tomorrow or next year or after they get married or after their career takes off, but repentance is a gift from God. When we feel the Holy Spirit pulling us, we have to act on it. That's why the old folk used to say, "Every time I feel the Spirit moving in my heart, I will pray!"

The Bible warns us with the example of Esau who despised the blessing of God. He had rejected God so many times that he willingly sold his birthright blessing to his brother for a bowl of beans. *"Make sure that no one is immoral or godless like Esau, who traded his birthright as the firstborn son for a single meal. You know that afterward, when he wanted his father's blessing, he was rejected. It was too late for repentance, even though he begged with bitter tears"* (Hebrews 12:16-17). That is why we have to seek the Lord while He is found. *"For God says, 'At just the right time, I heard you. On the day of salvation, I helped you.'* ***Indeed, the 'right time' is now. Today is the day of salvation***" (2 Corinthians 6:2).

HIDING PLACE

David's words invite us to pray and then give praise. David began to praise and worship the Lord this way, *"For You are my hiding place; You protect me from trouble. You surround me with songs of victory"* (Psalm 32:7). He called God his hiding place. This is a reference to ancient cities of refuge. Those were places where a wrongdoer could find safety. If you killed someone, it was the duty of the next of kin to kill you. The next of kin was called the avenger of blood. He would seek revenge and justice for the death you caused. With a hot heart and a sharp sword, he came looking for you. But in mercy, the Lord commanded Israel to have six cities of refuge. This was a place you could run to and find safety from the avenger of blood. The roads were paved and always well maintained. They were the best roads in Israel because the Lord wanted you to be able to run to safety. He didn't want you to have problems finding your hiding place. You could stay in the city of refuge until your trial, until they could investigate what really happened.

David understood that God was his hiding place, his city of refuge, when people were out to get him. He could find shelter in God when they called for his resignation. If the avenger of blood was hot on his trail, or if others tried to take David's life, he found that God would protect him. Not only was God a protector, but also He was David's judge and lawyer. God cleansed him from his iniquity and sin so that those who accused him no longer had a case against him. Even Satan had to step back because David was safe in the arms of God!

Not only was David safe and secure but also the Bible says he was surrounded with songs of victory. God surrounding us with songs of victory is surprising. When

I run into a fortress or seek refuge, I am running there to be safe. I am trying to get away from the avenger of blood, the adversary that seeks my life. My first thought is if I am going to be surrounded with something, surround me with walls or minefields or big guns. I would want God to bring out the tanks and the heavy artillery. The Bible says God doesn't build up a wall of bricks and mortar. He doesn't call for the angels that are full of strength. He doesn't even mobilize an army. He doesn't surround you with the things man surrounds himself with to feel safe. He surrounds you with what He knows will defeat your enemy. God surrounds you with a wall of worship. *"The weapons we fight with are not the weapons of the world. On the contrary, they have divine power to demolish strongholds"* (2 Corinthians 10:4, NIV).

The Lord keeps the enemy out by using a song. The Bible says God will surround you with a wall of praise. The devil can't penetrate that. Why? God inhabits our praise: God fills praise with His presence. Where true praise is, God is there also. And the devil can't get past God. The devil may try singing to you the song of defeat. However, David lets us know that the ditty of defeat has been replaced by verses of victory.

God is looking for us to honor Him with our decisions. He is looking for us to give up control of our life, and to turn from the wrong decisions that pull us from Him. He wants us to acknowledge our sin and confess it, and He has promised that He will be faithful to cleanse us and forgive us. After all that He has done for us, it is only fitting that we thank Him. We can praise Him for what He has done in the past and what He is doing in our lives and for the brilliant plans He has for our future.

Don't be afraid to share what God is doing in your life. David said, *"Give thanks to the LORD and proclaim His greatness. Let the whole world know what He has done"* (Psalm 105:1). Tell others of how God is moving in your life. The last thing you want to do is be an under-cover brother or sister.

Dear Lord, thank You for all that You have done in my life. I acknowledge that I have done wrong, and I am sorry for it. I don't want that sin to be a part of my life anymore. Allow me to experience the joy and peace of forgiveness through Jesus Christ.

CHAPTER 7

UNDERCOVER BROTHER

He was an undercover brother. His name was William Webb, the James Bond of his day. Webb was a freeborn black man, who was pale enough to pass for a white man and that's what he did. He transformed himself into a white man, and then he spied, snooped and swiped secrets for the Underground Railroad. In the dark of night, he would go to bars and taverns, and listen to drunk slave catchers to see how much they knew and what they were planning. With this information, he would then help lead slaves to Canada. He lived a dangerous life as an undercover brother, but it was a small price to pay to set the captives free.

Nicodemus, too, was an undercover brother, but unlike Webb, he was far from free. He was a powerful and respected man, a moral man and a member of the Sanhedrin or the Jewish Ruling Council. He was a wealthy rabbi and not the kind of man you would expect to see slipping from under the sheets with his wife and roaming the streets in the wee hours of the night.

He was creeping—not on his wife—but on everything he had believed and had known to be true. Nicodemus was having doubts about what he was teaching and living. Emptiness filled his heart, and he longed for more. He wanted more than he found in the synagogue or the council, more than he found in his marriage or his money. He was curious about that carpenter called the Christ. This undercover brother was on a mission, and so under the cloak of secrecy, he came to Jesus late one night.

Nicodemus waded through the darkness, searching for the Light. He probably came to Jesus to talk about the Kingdom of God. The Pharisees were all about the kingdom. They wanted to overthrow the current government and start their own, but they had no way of doing it. Jesus had the respect and the attention of the people, and Pharisees had the know-how in politics. If they joined forces together, they believed they could get a new government going!

"Unless you are born again," Jesus told him, "you cannot see the kingdom of God." Jesus was not interested in discussing prophecies and politics. He wasn't even interested in discussing signs and wonders. Jesus was interested in one thing—Nicodemus' relationship with God.

Jesus said you have to be born again, anew. You have to be transformed. Jesus knew that man was in a state of sin. Humans suffer from a terminal illness called iniquity. People think sin is an action, but sin is a condition. It is not just lying or stealing, but it is the disease that makes you want to lie or steal. Our condition was so bad that God came to the conclusion that we were beyond repair. There was no treatment that would cure the sinful heart. We would need a completely new one.

We were like an old broken–down car, where the mechanic throws up his hands and says, "This car is so messed up. It is so broken down that there is no sense in trying to fix it. You just need a new car." Jesus didn't come to repair humanity. He didn't come to fix you and me. He came to make us over, to make us new. Jesus came so that we could be born again.

The problem is, we have been trying to fix ourselves. I wish that I could give you three ways, seven keys, or twelve steps to transformation, but transforming yourself isn't something you can do. Transformation is something God does. It is something divinely mysterious.

INFORMED, CONFORMED, TRANSFORMED

We don't like the fact that our transformation is not completely within our control. To get around that, we try to create, duplicate, or at the very least imitate transformation. We do the same thing the Pharisees did. To cover up the fact that they had not been transformed, the Pharisees decided to be *informed.*

We think if we can have another Bible study, go to another service, or read another book, then no one will know that our hearts are full of hate. We think, *Nobody will know that I have a serious problem with lying. They will overlook my meanness and turn a blind eye to my pride if I am always being spiritually informed.*

It's not enough to be informed because knowing is only half the battle. You have to be transformed, so you can live out what you know. It's more than just knowing better; you have to be transformed by the power of the Holy Spirit, so you can do better.

Another way we try to hide the fact that we haven't been transformed is by being *conformed* to certain standards. Some church people don't go to R-rated movies, so you don't go to R-rated movies. They don't listen to a certain kind of music, so you stop listening to that kind of music. They dress a certain way, so you dress that way. I believe in Christian standards, but I don't want you to be fooled into thinking that because you have conformed on the outside that you've been transformed on the inside.

When you are undercover, you transform the externals. You are a master of disguises. You are constantly appearing to be one thing to the world around you, but on the inside, you remain unchanged. William Webb looked and acted like a white man on the outside, but he was a black man on the inside. When you are undercover, no matter what they call you or how they view you, when it's all said and done, on the inside, you are the old you.

Unfortunately, churches are filled with undercover brothers and sisters—people who only change on the outside. They try to look or to talk like Christians. These undercover brothers and sisters only make exterior changes. They haven't been *transformed;* they just conformed to what everyone else is doing. They are in a Christian community, but Christ is not in them.
"You must be born again," Jesus reminded.

Nicodemus, as educated as he was, acted like he didn't understand. He was being cynical. "Are we supposed to crawl back into our mother's womb and try it again?" he asked.

Jews and Greeks used the term "born again." Still, Nicodemus didn't understand Jesus because spiritual things are only understood through the Holy Spirit. Nicodemus was an educated man, but not a spiritual one. Jesus tried to break down what he was talking about. *"Jesus replied, 'I assure you, no one can enter the Kingdom of God without being born of water and the Spirit'"* (John 3:5).

BORN OF THE WATER

We must be born of the water. Water is important for at least two reasons. First, water represents life, both in the physical and the spiritual world. The majority of Earth is covered by water. The human body is mostly made up of water. It is what sustains you. Jesus describes water as living; there is something life giving in water.

Second, water is a purifying and cleansing agent. It washes the dirt from you. I am a firm believer that you need water to be clean. Sure, we have wet wipes and hand sanitizers. You can put sanitizing gel on your hands if you can't wash them, but your hands are not clean. They just host sanitized dirt. When you get water and wash your hands properly, you will see all the dirt that was on your "sanitized" hands. You need water to be clean.

Jesus said we have to be born of the water because we need to be cleansed. This is done through baptism. In baptism, you are washed and made clean, and ready to walk in the newness of life. Paul said, *"For we died and were buried with Christ by baptism. And just as Christ was raised from the dead by the glorious power of the Father, now we also may live new lives"* (Romans 6:4).

BORN OF THE SPIRIT

Many of us are baptized with water and we think we have arrived, but there is more to kingdom living. In baptism, you repent of your sins and are cleansed from them. Some think, *I am saved and that is it,* but the Christian life isn't just about securing a spot in heaven to live with God forever. Jesus came so that we would have abundant and eternal life. *"Now this is eternal life: that they know You, the only true God, and Jesus Christ, whom You have sent"* (John 17:3, NIV). Eternal life begins now through communion with the Holy Spirit.

Peter told the crowd on the day of Pentecost, *"Each of you must repent of your sins and turn to God, and be baptized in the name of Jesus Christ for the forgiveness of your sins. Then you will receive the gift of the Holy Spirit"* (Acts 2:38). Repentance alone is not enough. Repentance deals with your past, but the gift of the Holy Spirit empowers you for the future.

Admittedly, the Holy Spirit can be unsettling to us. The Spirit's activity is not something we can chart or explain. Sometimes, the Holy Spirit comes in and leaves more questions than answers. Jesus said, *"The wind blows wherever it wants. Just as you can hear the wind but can't tell where it comes from or where it is going, so you can't explain how people are born of the Spirit"* (John 3:8).

The wind, like the Holy Spirit, is mysterious. When I was little, my dad and I went to Lake Erie. While we were there, the wind began whipping and whirling and making funnels over the lake. The funnels were huge and moved towards us. My dad threw me in the car and raced home. We sat in the bathtub for hours waiting for the tornado to pass. It never came. There was no tornado. The wind was doing its own thing on the lake, but since we didn't understand the wind, we were afraid.

That's what's wrong with some of us—we are afraid of the Wind. We don't understand the divine Wind of God, the Spirit of the living God, and so we want to hide. We don't want the Spirit to fall on us. When the Spirit does come, we don't know what to do because we can't control or predict the Holy Spirit. Don't believe it when people tell you, "When the Spirit comes on you, you will be in complete control." When God comes into your life, He moves you out the way and takes over the controls. God is not interested in being the co-Pilot of your life. He wants to run it Himself—His way and His time. He is in control, not us!

In Acts 19, Paul meets some believers who were baptized by John the Baptist. They participated in the baptism of repentance, but Paul still noticed something was missing in their lives—the power of the Holy Spirit. They had not even heard of the Holy Spirit. Paul shared with them the story of redemption. He told them how Jesus lived and died and rose from the dead. Paul let them know before Jesus went to heaven He promised we would not be alone because He would send the Holy Spirit to guide our hearts and minds. They were re-baptized in this new knowledge. They were baptized with water, and then through the laying on of hands, they were baptized in the Spirit. The Holy Spirit came upon them equipping them with gifts to further the gospel.

It was not enough for them to repent and be baptized with water, but they had to be baptized with the Holy Spirit. The Spirit's presence and power were then clearly seen in their lives. Today, we need to pray for the same thing. The Bible commands us to be filled with the Holy Spirit (Ephesians 5:18).

Dear Lord, baptize me with the Holy Spirit! I need fresh wind and fresh fire to invade my life. I need an invasion, a takeover, a transformation! Let Your Spirit control my life. Lord, I don't want to be an undercover brother or sister anymore. I want to be the same, inside and out. Yank me out of the darkness and allow me to walk in Your marvelous light. I want to be born of the water and of the Spirit. I want to be born again.

CHAPTER 8

WHO'S YOUR DADDY?

On our birthdays, we are born into our families. We don't really have a choice in the matter. We don't choose our moms or dads. We don't choose where we live or how much money we have. We just kind of appear.

Kids can be cruel. When I was growing up, some kids were teasing one of my friends because he was adopted. I remember my father reassuring him, "You see all these kids," pointing at me and the others around, "we just got them. We didn't have a choice. We're stuck with them, but your parents chose you. You are special. They picked you out of all the other kids in the world. They chose you!" I remember standing next to my father thinking, *Man, I wish I was adopted.* I wanted someone to choose me.

The truth of the matter is we are all like that. We want to be chosen. I remember being in school and dreading the selection of the teams for dodge ball or kickball or whatever game we were playing. I was not very athletic, so unless my best friend was the captain, I was not picked first. I don't know if you remember the anxiety of waiting to hear your name, hoping to be chosen, but I remember it well.

The Bible describes a selection session that took place in Israel. Samuel, the prophet, came to Jesse's house to anoint one of his sons to be king over Israel. All the sons got ready. It was a huge event and they prepared a big feast. Everyone was present—everyone except David. This was before he became the famous King David. At this time, he was just a stinky shepherd boy. Nobody invited David. Nobody mentioned David.

His brothers were strong and handsome. The prophet knew any one of them would make a good king, but God hadn't selected any of them. "This is embarrassing. God hasn't chosen any of these to be king. You don't have anymore sons?" asked Samuel.

"Well, the youngest is out in the field," Jesse confessed. "Well, go get him," Samuel urged.

They sent for David and he quickly obeyed. I have always wondered how David felt walking into the house. I'm sure it was very evident that they were having a big party and that David's invitation was an afterthought. His father was hosting a great ceremony and they left David outside with the animals. His father was told to bring all his sons, and Jesse didn't even think to invite David.

It was apparent that David wasn't on anyone's mind. Still, he was on God's mind, and that was enough. David learned at an early age, *"Even if my father and mother abandon me, the LORD will hold me close"* (Psalm 27:10).

CHOICES, CHOICES

God chose David and God chose you. He wants you to be His son, His daughter. God is unlike any parent you have had or met. God breaks parent rule number one and lets His children select their parent. God will not force Himself on you. He chose you, and He patiently waits for the moment when you will choose Him. *"Here I am! I stand at the door and knock. If anyone hears my voice and opens the door, I will come in and eat with that person, and they with me"* (Revelation 3:20, NIV).

So no matter what kind of parents you had growing up, God is different. God is not abusive or absent, not low down, or on the down low. He's not a rolling stone; but He is the Rock. Even if your parents were good, God is still different; in that God our Father is GREAT!

"But God showed His great love for us by sending Christ to die for us while we were still sinners" (Romans 5:8). While we were enemies of God, He showed us how much He loved us. We can understand when parents risk their lives for their children, or when someone lays it all on the line for a spouse or a close friend. That seldom happens for an enemy.

With this, God showed us that He is in a class by Himself. God sent Christ to die for you while you were still His enemy in the hopes that you would become a part of His family. If God treats His enemies with such love, imagine how He treats His children? *"See how very much our Father loves us, for He calls us His children, and that is what we are!"* (1 John 3:1).

Through Christ, God adopted us and made us His children. The Bible reminds us of this over and over again. When you accept Jesus Christ as your Lord and Savior, you become a child of God. John 1:12 says, *"But to all who believed Him and accepted Him, He gave the right to become children of God."* When you receive Christ, you become a part of the family of God. *"And I will be your Father, and you will be My sons and daughters, says the LORD Almighty"* (2 Corinthians 6:18).

It all sounds too good to be true! You may be wondering, *"How could He love me after how I treated Him? How could He love me when I don't love Him like I should? How could I still be His child?"*

The Bible tells us, *"And I am convinced that nothing can ever separate us from God's love. Neither death nor life, neither angels nor demons, neither our fears for today nor our worries about tomorrow—not even the powers of hell can separate us from God's love"* (Romans 8:38).

Nothing can separate you from the Father's love. You are a child of God. It is not based on what you have done, but it is based on what was done for you. The blood of Jesus brought us all together in the family of God. We are related by the blood.

Have you ever watched one of those talk shows where they do a paternity test to determine the identity of the father? People have all kinds of stories and excuses of why they are sure that the father really isn't the father. The kids don't look like him. The mother was with another man. Perhaps, she never really loved him. But at the end of the day, it doesn't matter what anyone says, whether the kid looks or acts like the dad, whether the mom is acting right or not. At the climax of the show, the DNA test reveals whether the father is related to the child. It is not based on how someone feels, or what they have done; the proof is in the blood.

This is good news because there will be some times when we may not feel close to God, and we wonder if we are still His child. Be assured my sister and my brother that when you accept Jesus, you are a child of God and nothing can change that.

We all know that just because we are related to people does not mean you like everything your family does. Everybody has at least one crazy family member: an eccentric aunt, a crazy cousin, a weird uncle. As soon as you read the sentence above, someone came to mind. You knew who I was talking about. (Of course, if nobody came to mind, I am probably talking about you!)

Just because God is our Father does not mean He likes everything we do. I haven't met a parent who likes everything their children do, nor have I met children who like everything their parents do. Because God is our Father, He will correct us. He loves us just the way we are, but He loves us too much to leave us the way we are.

Parents want their children to grow up and be the best man or the best woman they can be. God wants nothing less. Unlike most parents, however, God has all the resources to make that desire a reality. *"And I am certain that God, who began the good work within you, will continue His work until it is finally finished on the day when Christ Jesus returns"* (Philippians 1:6).

God can make a miracle out of you. He can take you and make something beautiful of your life no matter how your life began. Even if you had a bad beginning, with God, you can still have a happy ending. The Bible says, *"The end of a thing is better than it's beginning"* (Ecclesiastes 7:8). When you enter into partnership with God, what's to come is better than what's been.

THE LOVING FATHER

When Jesus was on earth, He told a great story to illustrate what the Father was like. It is found in Luke 15. Many people call Jesus' story, "The Story of the Prodigal Son," but it is really, "The Story of the Loving Father." It's the story of a father, who had two sons. In so many words, the youngest son told his father, "I wish you were dead, so I could have my inheritance and get away from you. As a matter of fact, let's pretend for both our sakes that you are dead. Give me what is mine, and we can part ways forever."

I can't imagine the pain a parent would feel having this conversation with a child. Still this father, in all his love, gave the boy his inheritance. With a tear–stained face, he watched his young son pack up his stuff and leave.

The boy went far, far away. He bought himself a new wardrobe and wore the finest clothes. He threw the greatest parties and he always had people around him who liked being close to him. They loved him as long as he had money. He spent the money so fast; soon he had nothing left.

He wasn't worried because he had friends that he helped when they needed him, and he was sure they would return the favor. But he found out that they wouldn't even return his calls or texts! Then his phone got turned off. He went to look for a job, but he couldn't find one.

On the bright side, he was still the best-dressed bum in town. That bought him a few dinners and a place to stay a couple nights until the ladies figured out he was broke, unemployed, and homeless. He eventually had to sell everything. He was trying to make it, but he couldn't. It seemed like everything was failing.

He finally found a job feeding pigs. It wasn't a nice zookeeper job. It was more like a "dig in the trash until you are funky and dirty and find the pigs something to eat" job. And even though the pigs were eating trash and mess, he was jealous of them because they looked better, smelled better, and ate better than him.

That's when it hit him. He remembered who he was. "Who's your daddy? Why are you sitting here jealous of pigs? Don't you know who you are?" He remembered his father. The Bible says, "He came to himself" (Luke 15:17).

Then he remembered their last conversation. He remembered telling his father he wished he were dead. He divorced himself from being his son. He knew he didn't have a father anymore. A tear stung his cheek, but hope pricked his heart, "Even if I'm not a son—if I could be a servant—I would still be living better than this."

He now had a plan. He would go back home, and ask his dad—well, the man formerly known as his dad—for a job. He began the journey back, not knowing how it would end, but it was worth a shot. His walk was different. His steps were full of anxiety. There was no swagger, only sorry.

He made it into town, and he knew he would be home soon, but before he could get there, someone was running towards him. He knew that old limp anywhere. He was responsible for it. When he and his dad used to play basketball, he would break those ankles every game. He laughed to keep from crying.

As his dad got closer, he had this look in his eyes he had never seen before. His arms were out kind of funny. He flinched because he thought his dad was about to hit him, but instead he hugged him. He hugged Him. They embraced and those big, manly men cried.

"Dad, I'm sorry. I messed up big. I sinned, and I know I am not worthy to be called your son—"

This is where the father speaks, almost as if he didn't hear his son's words. "Bring my designer suit! Bring my ring and put it on his finger! Put some good shoes on his feet! And fire up the barbeque because we are about to have a party! This—MY SON—is home. He was dead, but now he's alive!"

Whoa! The son was not expecting that. I am sure he wondered how he could still be his son, after what he said, after what he did. That's just it. Their relationship was not based on what he had done, but it was always based on the blood. His father looked him in the eyes, with his hands on his son's shoulders and reassured him, "As long as my blood runs through your veins, you will always be my child."

I don't know if you caught it, but everything the son looked for in the far country—designer clothes, parties, people who loved him—he found not out in the world but in the father's house. The father was simply waiting for his child.

Christ has been waiting for you. I pray that as we have been on this journey together, you have found Him. I pray that you have made the decision to be born again into the family of God. The Bible says that if we are His children, then we are His heirs. That means we have a godly inheritance, love overflowing, joy unspeakable, peace beyond understanding, righteousness like a river, forgiveness like a flood, and hope springing eternally. Everything you need is in the Father's house. It is not based on what you do, but it is based on what He did. You are connected by the blood.

Dear God, thank You for allowing me to be a part of the family of God. Thank You for not looking at what I have done, but rather at what Jesus has done for me. Thank You for the blood of Jesus, that makes me Your child. I want to be Yours forever.

CHAPTER 9

WELCOME TO THE FAMILY

The Apostle Paul told those who accepted Christ, "So now you Gentiles are no longer strangers and foreigners. You are citizens along with all of God's holy people. You are members of God's family" (Ephesians 2:19). As members of God's universal family, it is my prayer that you will find a local faith family where you can be a part. Many call them churches. That is fine, but "church" means a lot of different things to different people.

Often when people say church, they actually mean a building, and they want to know what building you attend. Sometimes they think of it as a service, and they want to know what time it ends. When we use that term, we seldom mean the people of God. But in the Bible, "church" always referred to a group of people. Whether they were in the temple, in a house, by the riverside or hiding in catacombs, the place was irrelevant. It was all about the people.

That's why I like the term faith family. It communicates that we are talking about a group of people who are tied together by a common faith and common blood—the blood of Jesus. That is the unifying factor that makes us one. For many people, church ends after a couple of hours. But family doesn't end—family is forever.

If you don't have a local faith family, make sure you find one. It is God's desire for us to grow up in families, both biologically and spiritually. We are all supposed to have a personal relationship with Christ, but it is by no means a private one. We were created to grow in community.

It is my prayer that as we have been on this journey that you have not only found Christ, but that you have found in Christ, forgiveness and a new start. God has wonderful things in store for you if you stay close to Him. I pray that you experience every one of them.

Dear God, thank You for welcoming me into the family of God. Please help me to find a local faith family that I can worship with regularly that will help me to grow in Christ. Help my journey not to end here. Since I have found Christ, I know the journey has just begun.

ENDNOTES

[i] "Think Locally to Survive Globally," *Marketing Week* (May 31, 2001): 67-70, http://search.proquest.com/docview/228128091?accountid=11008.

[ii] David Ricks, *Blunders in International Business,* 3rd ed. (Malden, MA: Blackwell Publishing, 1999), 38.

[iii] Ibid., 88.

[iv] Festo Kivengere, *Revolutionary Love* (Fort Washington, PA: Christian Literature Crusade, 1983), 13.

[v] Diana R. Garland, *Family Ministry* (Downers Grove, IL: Inter Varsity Press, 1999), 13.

NOTES

NOTES

SPIRIT REIGN
PUBLISHING
A Division of Spirit Reign Communications